# HISTORY AROUND YOU

# 1

## D. Thornton

### Series editor
### A. WAPLINGTON

Oliver & Boyd

# Time Line

This chart shows some of the things you have read about in this book and what people looked like then.

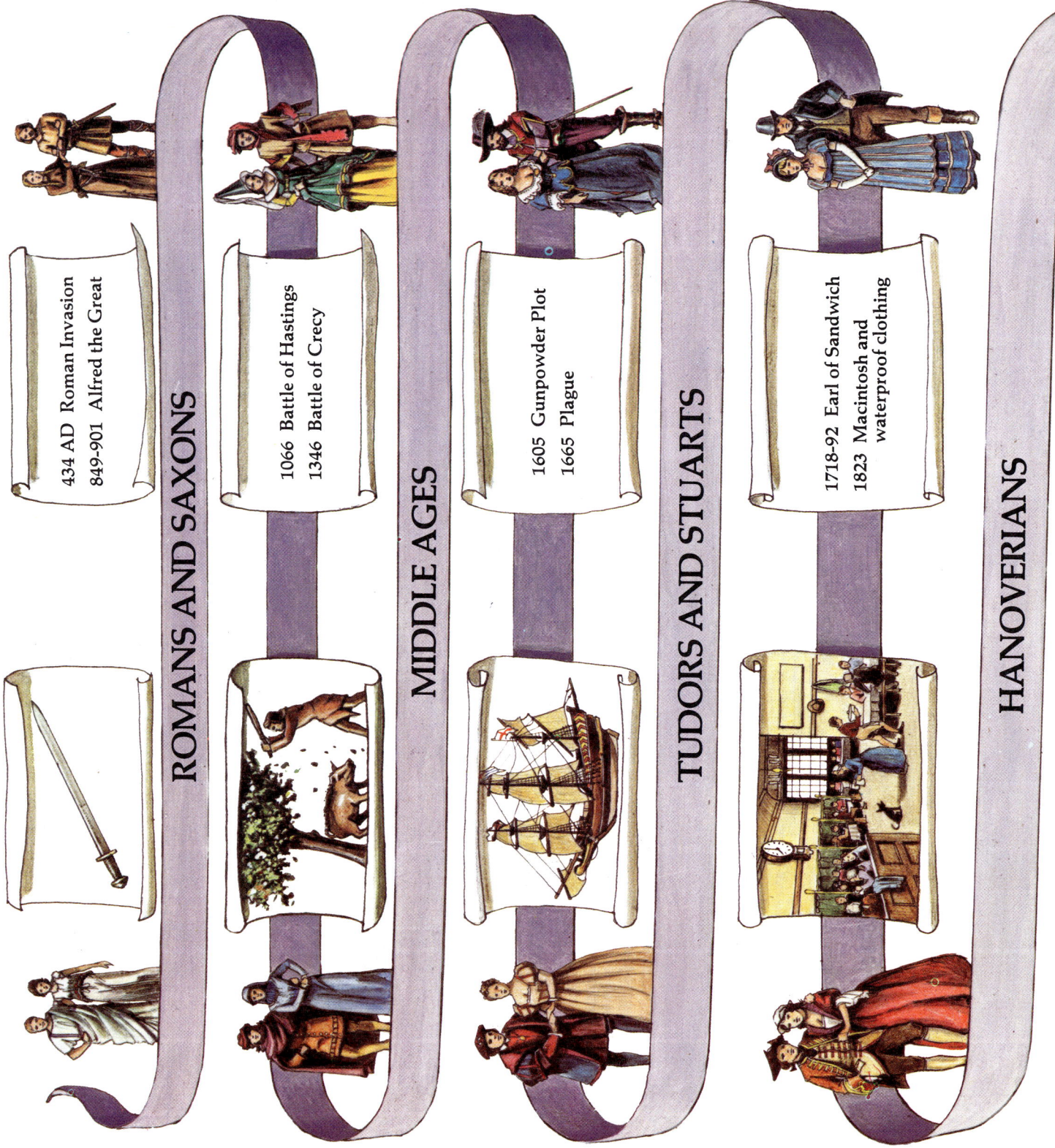

## ROMANS AND SAXONS

434 AD  Roman Invasion
849-901  Alfred the Great

## MIDDLE AGES

1066  Battle of Hastings
1346  Battle of Crecy

## TUDORS AND STUARTS

1605  Gunpowder Plot
1665  Plague

## HANOVERIANS

1718-92  Earl of Sandwich
1823  Macintosh and
waterproof clothing

VICTORIA

1840  Penny Post
1854-6  Crimean War
1899-1902  Boer War

EDWARD VII

GEORGE V

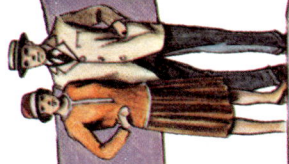

1928  Fleming & Penicillin
1930  Amy Johnson's flight

EDWARD VIII

GEORGE VI

1939-45  Second World War
1969  Man on the Moon
1971  Decimal Money

ELIZABETH II

# Introduction

Young people are often frustrated with traditional History syllabuses because they begin in the remote past and never seem to get to the present. This series begins with the pupils' present world and experiences and uses these as 'signposts' to lead them to an understanding of how people lived in the past, and to an understanding of the ways in which the past has influenced life today. So the arrangement of content in the series is broadly concentric. Book 1 starts with the immediate home environment, Book 2 the wider environments of the town, and Books 3 and 4 with places which pupils are more likely to encounter on journeys, school visits and holidays. Of course no arrangement of content, however appropriate, can guarantee quality of learning. As well as the language level, which has been carefully controlled, the learning experiences in the series have been chosen to develop skills and concepts which are important to an understanding of history but above all important to the pupils' general understanding of the world about them. The main objectives are:

1. The development of imagination. This is important because pupils need to understand people and what motivates them.
2. The ability to understand evidence. The earlier books concentrate on what is evidence, and drawing conclusions from evidence. Later books include a wider variety of evidence and cases in which evidence seems to conflict.
3. The development of an understanding of concepts, particularly similarity/difference and change/continuity. These concepts are vital to an understanding of a world which is 'shrinking' and changing rapidly.

A final word needs to be said about the arrangement of work within each book. We have kept very much in mind the needs of the classroom teacher able to devote roughly one session a week to history teaching. Each topic within a book provides a core of information, experiences and exercises for a class to work at. We have, however, written the basic core so as to stimulate pupils (and teacher) to take the study much further, and we have provided plenty of suggestions as to how this can be done.

So our aim is that, in following this series, young people will, in Robert Douch's words 'be involved in history, to see it, not as a film which they simply watch, but as a continuing play in which they themselves are actors.'

*Allan Waplington*

# Contents

In this book you will see some words with a line underneath. You can find out what these words mean by turning to the Glossary on pages 61, 62 and 63.

(Words in the Glossary which first appear in extracts are not underlined.)

# Clues

Sherlock Holmes was a famous detective in stories written by Conan Doyle. Like all detectives, he used to look for clues.

You can be a detective, too, and look for clues.

This bag was found the other day. Look carefully at the picture of what was in it. These things will give you clues about who owns it.

Is the owner a boy or a girl? What are the owner's hobbies? Do you think the owner is helpful to others? Would you say the owner is untidy? Would you say the owner is careless?

You will find the answers on page 8.

In this book we are going to look at many things. They will give us clues. The clues will tell us about the past.

## A Clue from the Sky

This photograph was taken from an aeroplane. People noticed the strange criss-cross lines, and wondered what they were. Archaeologists found out. The lines were clues to what was in the fields a long time ago. They were the streets of the old Roman town of Silchester.

Howard Carter

# A Great Discovery

Howard Carter was an archaeologist. He looked for things from the past by digging in the ground.

For many years he had been looking in Egypt for the tomb of a ruler, Pharaoh Tutankhamun. The Pharaoh lived many thousands of years ago, and Howard Carter needed a clue to show where the tomb was.

At last Howard Carter's men had some luck. They found a stone step. They were excited. The step was a clue. Carter knew that the step might lead to a stairway. The stairway might lead to a door. Would it be the door of the lost tomb? Carefully, the workmen removed the earth.

Sure enough, there was a door. They forced it open.

Behind the door was the richest treasure ever found anywhere in the world. It was indeed the tomb of Tutankhamun.

(above) The solid gold mask that covered Tutankhamun's face.

Statues guarded the Pharaoh's tomb.
The ancient Egyptians thought of them as goddesses.

# A Twentieth-Century Discovery

Alexander Fleming was a famous scientist. He was trying to discover something that would kill germs.

One day he had some special germs on a dish. A tiny speck of mould, like the mould on stale bread, fell onto the dish.

Alexander Fleming

Look at these dishes. What has happened to the germs on the second dish?

The clue Alexander Fleming spotted helped him to discover penicillin.
Today penicillin is used all over the world. Did you spot the clue? What was it?

Germs on dish.

Mould on dish.
It has killed the germs.

## Things to Do

**A** Imagine you are either Alexander Fleming or Howard Carter. Write or tell how you made your discovery.

**B** Here is a message in secret code. You will need a clue to understand the message. The second word is *like*.

> ### Answer to puzzle (page 4)
>
> The bag probably belonged to a girl, because there were some ballet shoes in it. Her hobbies were ballet, reading (the library ticket) and possibly drawing (the felt pens).
>
> She was helpful (the shopping list). Some people might say she was untidy because she still had the sweet papers. Others would say she was tidy because she had not thrown them on the floor. She was probably careless because she had lost her bag.

# Clues from the Past

It was Howard Carter's job to look for clues from the past.
Sometimes ordinary people find clues by accident.

## A Lucky Find

Nine-year-old Gary Fridd from Yorkshire found a clue. His class had been studying tadpoles. When they finished, the teacher asked Gary to take them back to the stream. He saw a piece of metal in the water. He pulled it out. It was an old sword. Gary took it home.

Experts said it was a Saxon sword. It had been made for a chief about the time when Alfred the Great was king.

Gary with his find.

## Carvings

Carvings on tombstones or buildings can often give us clues. This carving was made by the Romans. It shows a butcher's shop. There are things here that you can see in butchers' shops today. What are they?

9

## Clues in Museums

Another place where we can find clues about the past is a museum. This photograph was taken in the Abbey House Folk Museum in Leeds. Folk museums are specially made to show us how people lived in the past.

Sometimes whole houses and even streets are built in them. They show us what homes were like in times gone by. When this photograph was taken a man and woman dressed up to make the picture look more real.

What clue tells you that this photograph is a modern one?

This room is like the rooms in houses when Queen Victoria reigned. Do you think the family that lived here would be rich or poor? This is what a lounge or sitting room was like in those days. It was called the parlour. Houses in those days had lots of things in them. What is the most interesting thing here?

Some Victorians spent a lot of time in India. What makes you think the owner of this house may have been there?

Two of the paintings found on the walls of the caves at Lascaux.
They are some of the finest cave paintings ever found.

## Things to Do

**A** One day a group of French children went out to play. They lived near Lascaux. Their dog found a hole in the ground where a tree had fallen down. They went down the hole and found a cave. It was full of wonderful paintings. The pictures were painted by <u>cavemen</u> years ago. See if you can find out more about this discovery. Tell the story in a picture strip, using matchstick people.

**B** Imagine you are Gary Fridd. Tell the story of how you found your sword.

**C** Find a photograph taken before you were born. It might be a picture of where you live now. What changes do you notice?

**D** Look at the picture of the Victorian parlour on page 10. Find: an oil lamp, a piano, a bird in a cage, a fire screen, some flowers in a glass case, a photograph album.

**E** Where is the nearest folk museum to your home?

# Clues Around Your Home

We have seen some clues that help us to find out how people lived in the past. In this book we shall look for clues in our own homes. We might find the clues in old newspapers, or used stamps, or even in the words we speak.

All these clues will help us to find out about the past. History really is all around us.

Everyone has some sort of home. It might be a flat in a high-rise block, or an old cottage in the country. What sort of home do you live in?

Perhaps your home will have changed. If you look for the clues you will be able to see what it was like in the past.

## Changes in Houses

Look carefully at the pictures below. They show changes that have been made to an old home.

Try to spot the clues which will tell you what the house used to be like.

A new sliding door has been fitted to save space. What was here before?

What do you think used to be in this wall?

Why is there no chimney pot on the stack?

This house has been re-wired. Where was the electric plug before?

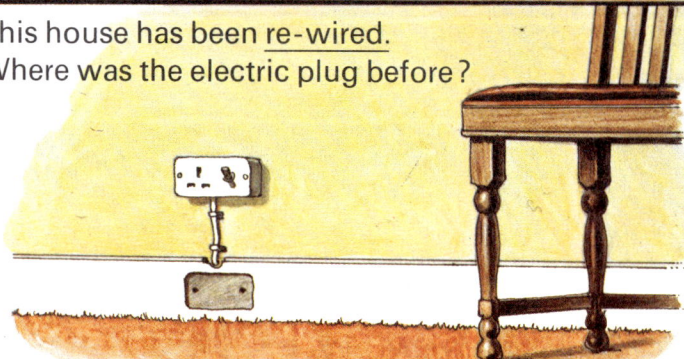

One of these houses has had an extension built on.
The top floor of the extension is another bedroom.
What do you think the part below it is used for?

## Things to Do

**A** Draw the parts of the house in the pictures on page 12 as they used to be.

**B** Here is a picture of an old kitchen. Make it into a modern one. Either draw a picture of it or make a cardboard model.

**C** Look at the outside of your home or some other building. Can you see any changes that have been made? Say what they are.

# The Day Before Yesterday

In this unit we shall look at clues that come from the 1960s. Perhaps you can find some clues like these in your home.

Sometimes people use old newspapers to line drawers. They may save them because they tell of something important.

When this newspaper was printed the men had landed on the moon but were still inside the lunar module.

Why do you think this newspaper was kept specially? If we look at it carefully, it will tell us a good deal about the 1960s. We can find out whether people used 'old' money or decimal money.

When did the first rocket with men on it land on the moon?

Neil Armstrong plants the United States flag on the moon, 21st July 1969.

## News Stories

Here are two news stories from the same paper. These stories are now history.

CAIRO : Egypt has decided to build another papyrus boat to complete the transatlantic mission which Norwegian explorer Thor Heyerdahl's vessel Ra failed to accomplish.

## planes shot down

CAIRO, Sunday
(Reuter)

SEVENTEEN Israeli aircraft were shot down in air battles today, according to Egyptian spokesmen.

PONTINGS

ALL WOOL CASUAL
KNITTED JACKET

13/M.46 — Look
ahead and buy
now for Autumn ;

W. size **52/6**

WX. OS **55/-**

Post &
pkg. 1/9.

Invaluable Classic
Jacket, light in weight
but warm ; washable. Beige,
Tartan Green, Navy, Peat
Brown or Cherry. (2nd choice
please.)

**Satinized Cotton**
**HOLIDAY DRESS**

2/M.543—Charming and very popular
square-neck, sleeveless style buttoning
down the side ; tie belt, pocket.
Assorted multicoloured floral and fancy
prints (example is typical), predominant
shades : Green, Flame, Blue or
Turquoise.

Hips 38, 40, 42, 44in. **35/-**

Outsizes (3/M.543), Hips 46, 48in **39/6**
Post & Pkg. 1/8.

MAYMAN
SEAMLESS FITTED CARPET LUXURY
BIG VALUE! LOW PRICES! SAVE £££'S!

CARPET A
9'x9' ROOM
FOR ONLY
**6** GNS

Here's new MAYMAN carpet from only 6/6 yd.—18" wide. One of
100's in the range of colours, patterns and qualities. Some in 100% Evlan,
others in blends of Evlan and Nylon. Wide choice of widths off the roll—
18", 27", 36", 54", 6', 7' 6", 9', 12', 15' and seamless carpet squares. MAY-
MAN makes it so easy for your family to enjoy the pleasure of luxury
deep-pile carpeting. Easy to cut and lay. Easy credit terms and money-
back guarantee.

## Advertisements

Advertisements tell us about what people bought.
Look at the advertisements above from the same
newspaper. Do you think the women's dresses
were like those they wear today?

The carpet cost 6 gns. This is short for guineas.
What does it mean?

Today we measure in metres and centimetres.
What did people measure in then?

**A** Use these words to fill in the blanks in the
sentences. Write out each complete sentence.

*motorways*       *cars*       *Northern Ireland*

*1969*       *Concorde*

1. The first man landed on the moon in ____.

2. The supersonic airliner ____ had its first
   flight in the 1960s.

3. ____ were built to provide fast roads.

4. Fighting started in ____ and many people
   were killed by bombs hidden in ____ and
   shops.

**B** Which countries were at war in 1969? Are
they still fighting?

**C** This is a record by the Beatles. They were a
famous pop group in the 1960s. Find out
about other records they made, and about
other entertainers at that time.

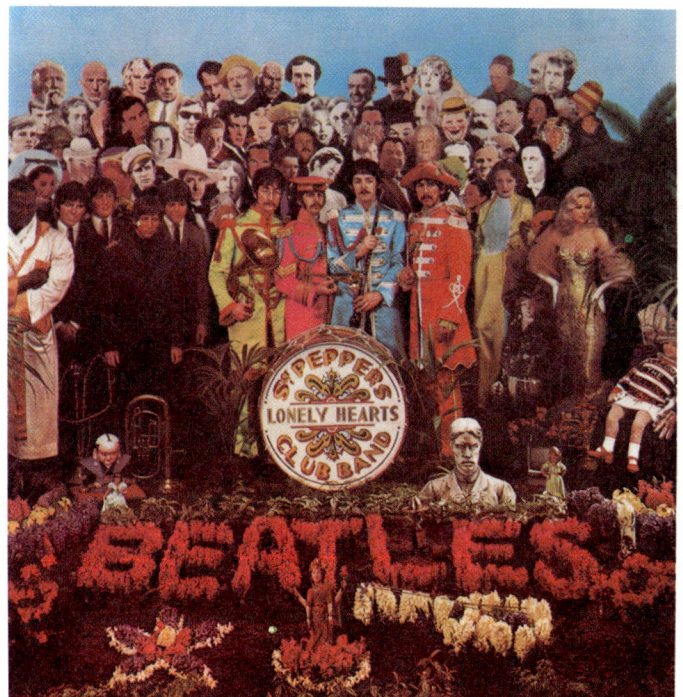

# The Second World War ~ the Home Front

Look carefully at these two bicycle lamps. What is different about the one on the left? Perhaps the picture below will give you a clue.

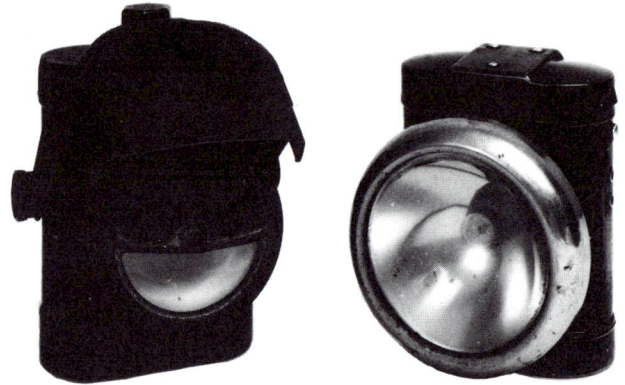

## Black Out

This picture was taken during the blackout in 1940. What do you think the blackout was for?

Pictures like this will remind older people of the Second World War. This war was fought against the Germans. It lasted from 1939 to 1945.

Many accidents happened to people in the blackout. Why do you think the men in the picture wore their shirts like this?

## Leaders

The Germans were led by Adolf Hitler. The British were led by Winston Churchill.

Churchill was the British Prime Minister from 1940.

Hitler came to power in 1933.

## The Forces

Young men and young women joined the Army, Navy or Air Force. Many of them went abroad to fight. At home people made guns and machines for the Forces.

## Air Raids

In Britain there were air raids, and enemy planes bombed many towns. In London the Underground stations were used as giant shelters. People sheltered there from the bombs dropped by the planes. Some people built their own shelters in the their gardens, like the one in this photograph.

## Gas Attack

The Government gave everyone in Britain a gas mask, because they thought the German Air Force might drop gas bombs.

Cards like this were given away in cigarette packets. This cigarette card shows how to take off a gas mask.

## Evacuees

Many children were taken from their homes to safer places in the country. They were evacuated from the cities. Here is a letter from one of these children.

The letter was written by a girl. She found life at Llanrug very different from Liverpool. What are the differences she wrote about?

> *My New Home*
>
> *My new home is Talsarn Farm Llanrug where I live with Mrs Lewis. It has a garden.*
>
> *The farm has two cows and two calves and hens. It is very different from our house in Liverpool because we have neither a garden nor a farm and the only animals we have are a cat and a dog.*
>
> *When we want water in Liverpool we only have to turn on the tap, but here we have to get a bucket and, like Jack and Jill, we go to fetch a pail of water but we don't fall down the hill.*
>
> *The only people who live in Talsarn are Mrs and Miss Lewis, but they are always in the farm. They come in and out with their clogs on and make a noise as if it were thundering.*

# Rationing

Here are some more clues from those days. One is an identity card and the other is a ration book. What do you think the ration book was used for?

There was only just enough food. It was rationed to let everyone have their fair share. Even sweets had to be bought with a ration book.

Why do you think everyone had to have an identity card?

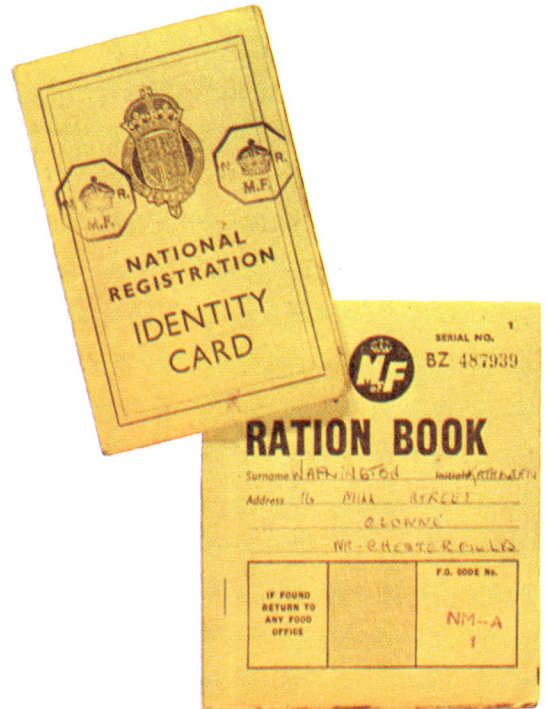

**A** Fill in the blanks from the words below.

*1939    spies    air raids    share*

Write out each complete sentence.

The war began in ____.

There was danger to people from ____.

People were given identity cards because there might be enemy ____ in Britain.

People also had ration books to ____ food out more fairly.

**B** Imagine you are a child who lived in a town. You have been evacuated to the country. Write a letter home to your parents about the things you found there.

**C** 'Dig for Victory' asked people to grow more food. 'Look out in the Black Out' warned people to be careful going out in the dark.
Design a poster for one of these messages.

18

# The Second World War ~ the Fighting Front

We must not forget that older people can often tell us what happened in the past. There are many people still living who fought in the war. They can tell us what they did.

## Souvenirs

Mr Fowler was in the Army during the war. Here are some medals that he was given. The first one tells us that he fought in Europe. The second one tells us that he was in the Army for the whole of the Second World War.

'I was also in Africa,' said Mr Fowler, 'but I must have lost that medal.'

## Dunkirk

In 1940 the British soldiers were helping the French and Belgians to fight the Germans. The British were pushed back to the coast. It seemed they would all be captured or killed. When people in England heard this, they sailed hundreds of small boats to Dunkirk in France to rescue the soldiers.

Mr Fowler was at Dunkirk. He said, 'It was very crowded on the beaches. We had to wait patiently in long queues. I was glad when it was my turn to get into a boat and come home.'

19

# Battle of Britain

The Germans attacked Britain with their Air Force. The Royal Air Force fought the enemy planes in the Battle of Britain. The Germans could not beat the RAF. They decided not to try to invade Britain.

German bomber shot down over England in 1940.

# The Invasion of Europe

Fighting still went on in Africa against the Germans and in the Far East against Japan. At last the time came when Britain and the United States of America decided to attack the Germans in Europe.

'Look at this money,' said Mr Fowler. 'They gave us this when we were going to invade in 1944.'

Special invasion money. What clues tell you where the soldiers were going?

NOTHING is to be written on this side except the date and signature of the sender. Sentences not required may be erased. If anything else is added the post card will be destroyed.

[Postage must be prepaid on any letter or post card addressed to the sender of this card.]

I am quite well.

I have been admitted into hospital

{ sick } and am going on well.
{ wounded } and hope to be discharged soon.

I am being sent down to the base.

I have received your { letter dated 8th & 9th
{ telegram "
{ parcel " 5th

Letter follows at first opportunity.

I have received no letter from you
{ lately
{ for a long time.

Signature only

Date 12-8-44

Forms/A2042/7. 51-4997.

Mr Fowler and the other soldiers could not write letters home. Instead they were given postcards like the one on the left. It was important that they did not tell anyone where they were going. Why do you think this was?

# D Day

Thousands of British and American troops landed in France on 6th June 1944. That day is called D Day. It is short for Deliverance Day.

The Germans were driven back from the coast of France. Finally, in May 1945, the Germans were beaten.

In August of that year the United States dropped two atomic bombs on the Japanese.

Japan surrendered and the Second World War was over.

D Day. These are special ships for landing soldiers and tanks on beaches. They are taking part in the biggest invasion by sea in the history of the world.

## Things to Do

**A** This unit has told us only about the British part in the war. Two other nations involved on the British side were the USSR and the USA. Find out what you can about what they did.

Here are the names of some famous battles to help you: *Pearl Harbour, Stalingrad, Midway*.

**B** Imagine you were a soldier at Dunkirk. Tell what you saw.

**C** Find out about these people:

*Winston Churchill*     *Douglas Bader*

*Leonard Cheshire*     *General Montgomery*.

**D** If you know anyone who was in the war, find out what they did. What did they wear? What did they do? Where did they go?

**E** Mr Fowler said, 'I joined the British Legion. We have parades every Poppy Day.' Find out what the British Legion is and what Poppy Day is about.

# The 1930s

**LIVERPOLITAN**

MAY 1936

AN ILLUSTRATED MONTHLY
REVIEW OF MERSEYSIDE AFFAIRS

PRICE 3D.

| LIVERPOLITANA. | A CENTURY of PUBLIC SERVICE | "BETWEEN OURSELVES" |
|---|---|---|
| A notable Liverpolitan MR. WILLIAM ARMSTRONG | The L. & L. & G. | A candid commentary on Merseyside affairs WEDDINGS — FASHION'S FANCIES |

ELECTRICITY YOUR SERVANT

**SELECTRICITY**
FOR SPRING CLEANING

EASIER CLEANING

IRONING

WASHING

BOILING

AMPLE HOT WATER & HERE'S TO A

GOOD SPRING CLEAN

This magazine was read in the 1930s. Which city was it read in?

Inside such magazines we can find lots of clues about the past.

It was then that aeroplanes and cars became more popular. For the first time many working people were able to go for a week's holiday.

People were beginning to use electricity for lighting in place of gas. They were even beginning to use gas or electric cookers.

Look at the advertisement. What was electricity used for then? What do you think the object on top of the washer was for?

# New Ideas

Many flying records were broken then. Amy Johnson took just under three weeks to fly from England to Australia.

How long does it take now?

The BBC began broadcasting in the 1930s.

Look at the photograph below. What are microphones like today?

Look at the clothes the announcer is wearing. Do announcers wear clothes like this today?

Amy Johnson. In 1930 she flew to Australia in an aeroplane like this. She was the first woman to fly there by herself.

Stuart Hibberd at the microphone. Later, during the Second World War, his voice became known to millions as a reader of the news.

1939 Daimler.

The motor car was still quite a new invention. Only a rich person would be able to buy a car like this. It cost about £500. A cheap car would cost £100.

A working man would earn about £2.50 to £3.50 a week.

## Having Fun

Many people went for a holiday for the first time. Usually they went to the seaside near where they lived. If you lived in Liverpool you might have crossed the River Mersey to New Brighton.

People would travel by steam train or coach. They would stay in a boarding house or caravan. What kind of things could they do on holiday in New Brighton?

N.B... COME TO NEW BRIGHTON

**NEW BRIGHTON**

*Near enough for a day visit is New Brighton*—but with so many attractions that a long holiday there never seems long enough.

Miles of golden sands face the sunlit waters of the Irish Sea. There are golf links, tennis courts, bowling greens and a magnificent bathing station; lovely parks where you may hear the finest military bands; a new £50,000 pier; illuminations; four miles of promenade; theatres, cinemas and dancing.

Corporation steamers leave Liverpool landing stage every few minutes. While you are here for the Pageant, spend at least one day in New Brighton—you'll enjoy every moment.

*There's sun and fun at*
**NEW BRIGHTON** (WALLASEY)
**25 MINUTES FROM LIVERPOOL**

## Things to Do

**A** Write down six things you have found out about the 1930s. Find an old magazine. Write down six things it tells you about when it was printed.

**B** Draw the objects on page 22. When you have done that, draw the same objects we use today.

**C** Imagine you are a child in the 1930s. You have been taken to the seaside for the first time. Write down what you saw and did. The advertisement for New Brighton may help you.

# Boyhood Memories

In Unit 6 we saw that we can find out about things in the past from older people. They can talk about what they remember. Mr Wainwright talked about his boyhood.

## School Days

He went to the village school. Below is his class photograph. Look carefully and see if you can spot him.

'The girls wore lace up boots and pinafores,' he said. 'You can tell which boys came from the better off families, because they wore sailor collars. The rest of us wore rubber collars. When we washed our faces,' he laughed, 'we washed our collars too!'

Why do you think the poorer boys did not wear sailor collars?

Mr Wainwright today.

Mr Wainwright's old school.
Is it like your school? Are there any differences? What are they?

25

# The Village

All his life Mr Wainwright has lived in the same village. 'When I was a boy there were lots of fields around our village. Nowadays houses have been built on them,' he said. 'It's sad to see them go, but people have to have homes, don't they?'

The old view painted by Mr Wainwright.
Notice the fields and house in the corner.

The view today.
Notice that the houses have no chimneys.

Why are there no chimneys on the houses in the right hand picture?

# The Village Band

'Our village had a band. My father played in it,' said Mr Wainwright. Which man in the photograph do you think was the leader of the band?

'People liked listening to the band,'

Mr Wainwright remembered. 'There was a bandstand in the park where they played on Sundays.'

Is there a park near you that had a bandstand? What was it like?

# The Village Church

'This is St Mary's Church at Middleton. I was a choirboy there,' said Mr Wainwright. 'In those days it used to have a spire. They had to take it down as it was not safe. It was the mining, you know.' How do you think that coal mining could have made the spire unsafe?

A  Mr Wainwright was at the right hand end of the back row in the photograph on page 25. How many boys came from better off homes? How many boys came from poorer homes?

B  Look again at the photograph on page 25. Draw a boy and a girl from those days. What things are different in your school? Write them all down.

C  Children in those days often used to play with hoops or at whip-and-top. Not many children play with them today. Why do you think this is?

D  Ask your grandparents or some older person about their school. Find out:

1.  What they wrote with.
2.  What kind of lessons they had.
3.  Whether there were school trips.
4.  If they remember any special things happening while they were at school.

# Family Album

Earlier units show how photographs can often give us clues. They can tell us how people dressed, where they lived and how they enjoyed themselves.

Photography started to be popular when Victoria was Queen. This photograph was taken then. It was taken in a studio. Very few people could afford to buy their own cameras in those days.

The people in the photograph below are going for a trip in a charabanc. Can you spot: a horn, the lights and a spare wheel?

What would the charabanc driver do if it started to rain? Look at the back for a clue.

Look at the tyres. Why do you think the people might have had a rather uncomfortable ride?

# Through the Years

Photograph 1 of four brothers was taken during the Second World War. Which brother do you think had an important job in a factory? Which man was in the Army, which was in the Navy and which in the Air Force?

1.

3.

Photograph 3 was taken ten years later. The boy on the bicycle is twelve years old. Is he wearing long or short trousers?

There were few supermarkets then. People mostly went to small shops near their homes. Can you see a corner shop here?

Photograph 2 was taken in 1948. What clue tells you that the war was only just over?

The boy is about twelve years old. Do boys of that age today wear the kind of trousers he is wearing?

2.

4.

Photograph 4 was taken in 1973. The people were on holiday. Was the photograph taken by the mother or the father of the family?

You will see that cars are quite different from the one on page 28.

*(Postcard — front/address side)*

34 High Street
North Shore
Blackpool,
August 4, 1915

Dear Miss Marshall
I hope you are
still keeping
well. And
I want to go
back to school
with love
Herbert Robinson.
xxxxx

POST CARD

The address to be written here

Miss Marshall
Wakefield
Road
Dewsbury
Yorks,

## Postcards

This postcard was sent by a schoolboy on holiday. How can you tell? What is the name of the king on the stamp?

August Bank Holiday in England used to be during the first week in August. Now it is in the last week. Was this postcard written in Bank Holiday week?

## Holiday Snaps

People like to remember their holidays, so they take photographs of them. Here is a picture a mother took of her husband and two children. She used a box camera. What kind of cameras do we use today? What other ways do people use to recall their holidays?

What tells you that this picture was taken many years ago?

# Objects from the Past

Many people save old things. Sometimes they buy them from <u>antique shops.</u> Mrs Lockwood bought an object like this in an antique shop.

'I might put some flowers in it,' she said. 'In the past people used to drink out of it. The piece of pottery across the top makes it very special.'

What do you think it was for? The faces of some of the men in the band on page 26 should give you a clue.

## Flag Days

This is a special kind of pin. Look at the photograph of the ladies. They are selling flags on the first flag day.

What do you think they would use a pin like this one for? Do you think it would be easy for them to keep their hats on?

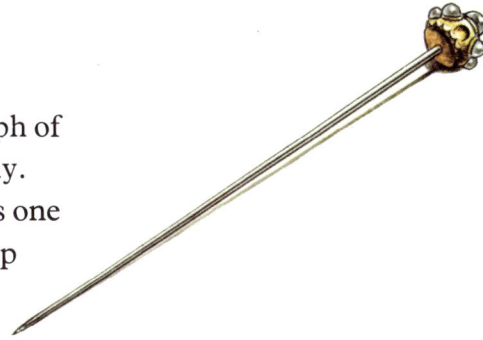

Ladies selling flags in London on the first flag day in 1912.
It was called Alexandra Rose Day after Queen Alexandra.

Sometimes a family will save something that is old. The objects on this page have been saved by two different families.

## Pattens

Mrs Osborn owns these now. 'My grandmother used to wear them,' she said. 'They are called <u>pattens</u>. Toddlers used to wear them to keep their feet out of the snow.'

What do children wear today to keep their feet dry?

The patten on the left is on its side so that you can see what the top looked like.

Family Register.

Joseph Bell born Nov 6th 1809
Ann Bell born June 26th 1812
Sarah Bell born November 17th 1840
Thomas Bell born February 19th 1843
The above Thomas Bell died June 6th 1843
Thomas Bell born June 28th 1844
Joseph Bell born September 4th 1846
Anne Bell born March 31st 1849
The above Joseph Bell died Febuarly 4th 1851
Eliza Bell born November 25th 1851
The above Anne Bell died June 25th 1853
Joseph Bell born Jany 15th 1855
Ann Bell Died Decr 22nd 1868 aged 56 years

## Family Bible

Many families used to keep a large Bible. This was called a <u>family Bible</u>. In it the names of the family were written down. The father wrote down when the children were born, or when anyone in the family got married or when they died. This Bible belonged to the Bell family.

Did people have large families then? Many of the children died. How do you know? Why do you think the baby born in 1844 was called Thomas?

People often called their children after famous men and women in the Bible. Did this family?

Can you spell the months of the year better than Joseph Bell?

# Pens

People like old objects so much that they even buy copies of them. This is really a ball point pen. It has been made to look like a quill pen. What do you think quill pens were made from?

To be able to write with one you need a sharp point. People used to sharpen their quills with special knives. They were called 'pen knives'.

## Things to Do

**A** Here are three objects. They were used in the past for:

> warming the bed
> sweeping the carpet
> making toast.

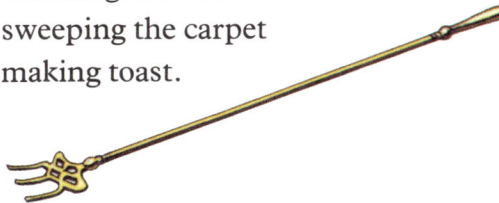

Which object did which job? Draw the objects that do the same jobs today.

**B** What are these five objects? Say what each was used for. To help you, here are nine suggestions. Only five of them are right.

*flat iron*          *paint pot*          *broad scissors*
*rounded knife*      *poker*              *lidded frying pan*
*shaving mug*        *curling tongs*      *door stop*
*warming pan*

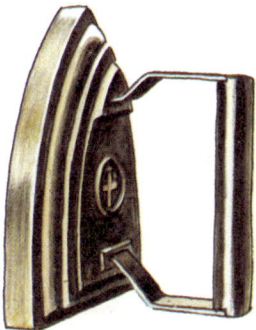

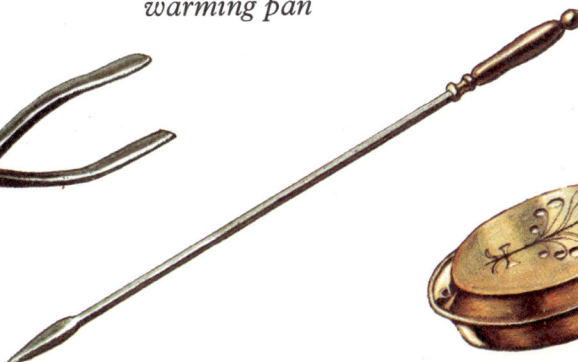

# Stamps

Do you collect stamps? They can give us clues about the past. Let us see what sort of things stamps can tell us.

## Early Stamps

The Queen on these two stamps is Queen Victoria. She was Queen in 1840 when the first stamps were used.

Later the sheets of stamps were perforated by a machine, as they are today. It is easy to tear stamps off the sheet as they are needed.

## Penny Post

At one time it was very expensive to send letters. They cost more the further you sent them.

Rowland Hill said it would be better to charge just one penny to send each letter. The Post Office did not think this was a good idea, but they tried it out in 1840.

It was a great success. Soon countries all over the world copied the idea of the Penny Post.

Penny Red

Halfpenny Red

Rowland Hill the 'father' of the Post Office

The mail coaches in this picture are about to go to south-west England. Notice the boy who has been brought by his father to watch them start off.

# Kings and a Queen

These stamps show the four kings and a queen who came after Queen Victoria. What are their names?

Can you find a stamp where the king is looking into the dark? Some people said that it was a sign of bad luck for him. Why do you think the crown on his stamp is over to one side and not above his head? See if you can find out what happened to this king.

# Special Stamps

Here are some commemorative stamps. Each one reminds us of a famous event or person. How can you tell that all these stamps are British?

Here are some questions. You can answer them by looking at the stamps on this page.

Which stamps remind us of things we have read about already in this book?

Which is the oldest person?

When did Elizabeth II become Queen?

When was her daughter married?

Which famous Prime Minister is shown on a stamp?

When were the Olympic Games held in England?

What year was Tutankhamun's tomb found?

Who made the first non-stop flight across the Atlantic?

# Overseas Stamps

Every country uses postage stamps. They have commemorative stamps too. Even their ordinary postage stamps tell us something of their past.

The old German stamp has Hitler on it. (See page 16.)

Why do you think the South African stamp is printed in two languages?

(See page 16.)

---

## Things to Do

**A** Think of an important event which happened this year. Write down what it is and design a stamp for it.

**B** Try to find out:

1. What is the Acropolis? (It is on the Greek stamp on this page.)
2. Who was George Washington?
3. Why was Malta given the George Cross?
4. Who was Florence Nightingale?

**C** Find out and tell the story of the post from its earliest days. Here are some words to help you:

| | | |
|---|---|---|
| *mail coach* | *post boy* | *highwayman* |
| *pillar box* | *Royal Mail train* | |

# Our Names

We have called this book *History Around You*. We must never forget that we, too, are a part of history. Everyone has an ancestor who lived at the time of the Battle of Hastings.

At first people had only one name. This was all right when the villages they lived in were small. It was confusing when the villages grew bigger.

Then people began to be given a second name. This helped to tell the difference between two people with the same first name.

## What People Looked Like

People were often given names which described what they looked like.

John had red hair. He was called John the Red. Over the years his name changed slightly, and today his descendants are called Read or Reid.

This is Edward Ball. His name has changed. What do you think his ancestor was called?

## How People Behaved

Names also tell us how people behaved. See if you can match these names to the drawings.

*Doolittle*          *Armstrong*          *Smart*

*Lightfoot*          *Longfellow*

## Where People Lived

Names might be taken from where people lived.

Here is a village in the Middle Ages. The names of the people who lived in the numbered houses are in the list below. Match the numbers to the names. (There are more names than you need.)

*Brown*   *Dawson*   *Miller*
*Cole*   *Green*   *Jones*
*Attwood*   *Wells*   *Bridge*
*Marsh*   *Fieldhouse*

## Names from Jobs

Look at these four men.
One is called Cooper.
One is called Wheelwright.
One is called Tyler.
One is called Fletcher.

Decide which is which. (You may need a dictionary to help you.)

Do you know anyone called Smith? It is a very common name. Each village used to have its own blacksmith. It is easy to tell where the name 'Smith' came from.

What were the jobs of the ancestors of people called Taylor and Cook?

38

# Names from Parents

It was confusing if father and son had the same name. The son of William became Williamson. It might even be shortened to Wilson.

In Ireland the son of Brien became O'Brien. What was the son of Donald called in Scotland? Many Scottish names begin like this.

**A** Write down the names from the list below to fit these meanings. You are given more names than you need.

1. means fair headed
2. a nickname for someone with a thirst
3. means someone who makes arrowheads
4. possibly someone who played that part in a play

*Fairweather   Arrowsmith   Fairfax   Shore
King   Drinkwater   Scattergood*

**B** Where do you think the names *Baker   Hutchinson   McNab* came from?

**C** Sometimes the spelling of a name has changed over the years. What names do you think these were?

   *Lang   Vidler   Lunnon*

**D** Make a list of the names of some of the people in your class. Write down where you think the names came from. (The book *Discovering Surnames* by J. W. Freeman, Shire Publications may help you.)

**E** We are all related to someone who has a different last or surname. Find out how many different names you are related to.

**F** Imagine you are living in the Middle Ages. What do you think you would be called? Draw a plan of your village and explain who lived in each house, what they were called and what their jobs were.

# Names We Know

We saw in the last unit how people's names give clues to the past. Some people have given their names to inventions or even food or toys.

## Teddy Bear

Everyone has heard of teddy bears. They were called after Theodore Roosevelt. He was an American President whose nickname was 'Teddy'.

One day he was out hunting. He found a bear cub. An artist drew a picture of him with the bear. At this time the small cuddly bears that we know were becoming popular toys. They became known as Teddy bears.

Theodore Roosevelt, President of the United States of America from 1901 to 1909.

## How the Sandwich got its Name

The Earl of Sandwich liked gambling. He lived about 200 years ago. One night he did not want to stop gambling, but he was hungry. He ordered his servant to put some meat between two slices of bread. Now he could eat and go on playing! The first sandwich was born.

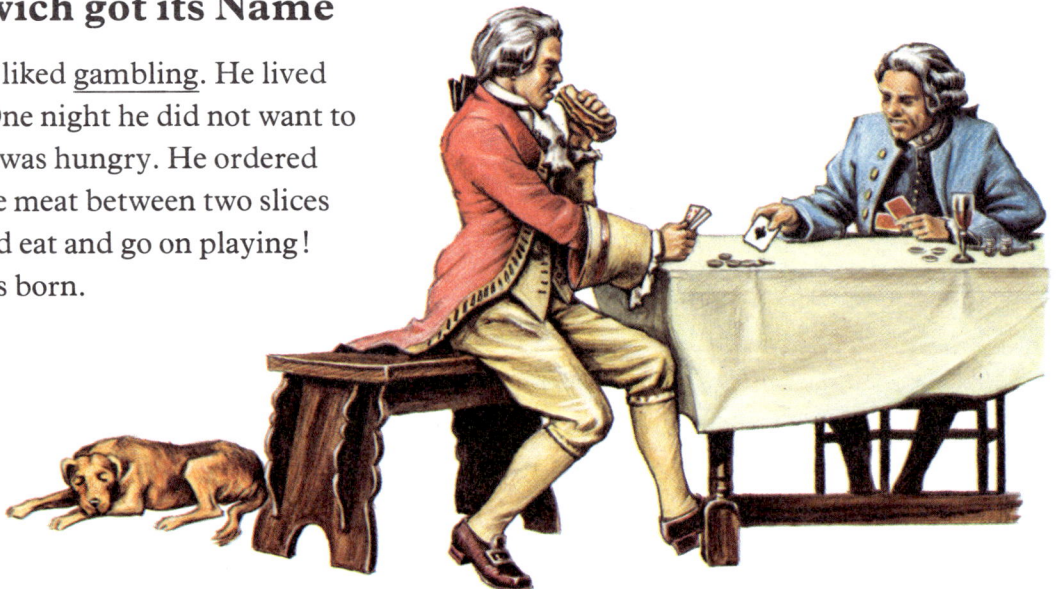

## Keeping Out the Cold

Many of the clothes we wear get their names from people or places.

The soldiers in the top picture are fighting in Russia at a place called Balaclava, during the Crimean War. It was very cold there in winter. When they were in camp, the soldiers wore special clothes to keep out the cold. Some of them had woollen helmets which covered the top of their heads and their ears. What do we call such helmets today?

It was during this war that Florence Nightingale became the first famous nurse. She took some nurses out to the Crimea to look after the soldiers who had been wounded during the Crimean War.

## Keeping Out the Wet

Charles Macintosh was a Scottish chemist. He wanted to make clothes that were waterproof. The first coats and capes he made smelled very badly, but they did keep people dry.

Today we all wear mackintoshes at some time. Over the years the spelling of the word has changed. How?

41

# The Hoover Cleaner

This is an advertisement for a <u>vacuum cleaner</u>. The first vacuum cleaner was made by an Englishman in 1901. An American firm, called Hoover, began to sell them in 1927. Today when people use a vacuum cleaner to sweep the floor, they say they are 'hoovering' it.

**AT PRE WAR PRICES** *(plus purchase tax)*

**THE HOOVER**
*The World's Best Cleaner*

**THREE CLEANERS IN ONE!**
○ **ELECTRIC CARPET BEATER**
○ **ELECTRIC CARPET SWEEPER**
and
○ **ELECTRIC VACUUM CLEANER**
*Easily convertible for cleaning upholstery curtains and for dustless dusting*

MODEL 375 £10 - 15 - 0 PLUS PURCHASE TAX £2 - 13 - 9

MODEL 262 £17 - 5 - 0 PLUS PURCHASE TAX £4 - 6 - 3

CLEANING TOOLS EXTRA

*ENQUIRE HERE FOR COMPLETE INFORMATION.*

## Things to Do

**A** The men listed below all gave their names to inventions or discoveries.

*Louis Pasteur*

*Alessandro Volta*

*J. L. McAdam*

*Samuel Plimsoll*

Find out what the inventions or discoveries were. You will find the *Children's Britannica* useful. The pictures give you clues, but not answers.

**B** Leslie Hore-Belisha was the Minister of Transport in 1934. He brought out a special crossing for <u>pedestrians</u>. A black and white pole showed people where the crossings were. The pole had an orange ball on the top. What do we call these poles?

# Nursery Rhymes

Sometimes even nursery rhymes can tell us about the past.

'Jack and Jill' is about children going to fetch water. People had to get their water from wells, or from ponds or streams. The children in the rhyme were probably going to a dew pond on top of a hill. Jack and Jill meant a boy and girl in Elizabeth I's time.

Water seller in the days of Elizabeth I. Much of the water in those days was polluted by rubbish.

## Fairs

'Simple Simon' tells us about going to the fair. People went to fairs to buy and sell things.

In this picture you can see a busy fair. What do you think some of the people are doing?

The fair at Pitlessie in Fife. Notice the soldier. What do you think he is asking the labourers?

## Hark, Hark the Dogs Do Bark

In the days of Queen Elizabeth I many people lost their farms. Rich men bought the land for sheep to <u>graze</u> on. Many of the poor farmers became beggars.

## Ring a Ring a Roses - The Plague

Say the rhyme 'Ring a ring a roses'. Some people think that this rhyme describes the <u>plague</u>. The plague was a terrible disease. It made people cough and sneeze, and a rosy rash appeared on their bodies. Finally they died. Sometimes people carried small bunches of flowers, called posies. They hoped that these would drive the disease away.

A London street during the plague. So many people died they were carried away in the 'death cart'. Notice the cross on the door to show there was plague in the house.

Beggars arriving in a town. What do you think might happen when they arrived?

# The Watch

In those days there were no policemen. How do you think people in towns kept a look out for trouble? Here is a nursery rhyme which may give you a clue.

Set a man to watch all night
Watch all night, watch all night
Set a man to watch all night
My fair lady

## Things to Do

**A** Write down the names of four nursery rhymes which tell you that people lived on farms or in the country.

**B** Sheep were very important in the past. Their wool was very valuable. Which nursery rhymes mention sheep?

**C** You live in a town and own a baker's shop. Tell what you did when you heard a crowd of beggars coming down your street.

**D** Imagine you are a person who has lost his farm and become a beggar. Write down what you do as a beggar.

**E** You have been taken to the fair in the picture on page 43. Tell the story of what you did and what you saw there. If you like, you could tell it in a picture-strip with matchstick people.

**F** Find out more about:
*the plague   the watch   street sellers children's jobs.*

# Eating and Drinking

These pictures were drawn in the Middle Ages.

Farmers did not have enough <u>fodder</u> to last their animals all through the winter. They fattened their pigs on acorns and then they killed them.

There were no fridges in those days to keep the meat fresh. Salt was rubbed into the meat to stop it from going bad. How do we keep food fresh today?

Why do you think the men are knocking the acorns off the trees?

The man on the left is about to kill the pig. What do you think the man on the right is doing?

## Frozen Food

Clarence Birdseye was an American. In 1912 he went to Labrador near the Arctic. He saw that food that was frozen lasted a long time.

When he got home he tried to find a way of freezing food quickly. At last he succeeded. Where do you find his name today?

A modern frozen food store. Clarence Birdseye's frozen food first went on sale to the public in 1929.

# In the Kitchen

Here is a kitchen scene from the Middle Ages. The man with the long spoon is basting the meat. The boy who is turning the handle of the spit is called a turnspit. Why do you think he was called this?

Bread and meat were the main foods in those days. But people ate apples and vegetables too.

Water was often polluted so even the children drank beer or cider.

Have you noticed that people did not drink tea or coffee or eat potatoes? Why do you think this was?

# The Potato

The potato was grown at first in South America. The Spaniards brought it to Europe about the time of Queen Elizabeth I. Potatoes had become very popular in Britain by about two hundred years ago.

# A Cup of Coffee

This is Lloyd's Coffee House in London. Friends used to gather together to discuss business. Insurance business was done here. Nowadays you may hear of ships being insured with Lloyd's of London.

Lloyd's Coffee House in London. Coffee was first brought to Britain about 1650.

## Toffee and Football

Molly Bushell lived in a part of Liverpool called Everton. She used to make toffee and sell it to people.

Today Everton football team is nicknamed 'The Toffees'.

The house of Molly Bushell, the Everton toffee-maker.

Everton footballers.

---

## Things to Do

**A** Imagine you are a boy or girl who lived in the Middle Ages. You work in the lord's kitchen. Describe what you do there.

**B** Ask an old person what kind of sweets they had when they were young. During the war sweets were rationed. Ask an older person what they ate instead of sweets.

**C** In the last unit you saw how nursery rhymes gave us clues about the past. Which nursery rhymes tell us about the food people used to eat?

**D** Find out from your school or class library when tea, cocoa and turkeys were first brought to Britain.

# Special Days

Every year we do special things at special times. We call these things customs.

## Christmas

Do you know how the custom of Christmas trees started?

Once a holy man called Boniface went to Germany. He went to preach about Jesus. He saw some <u>pagans</u> worshipping their god under an oak tree. Boniface chopped the tree down. He pointed to a tiny fir tree. 'This tree shall be your holy <u>emblem</u>,' he said.

From then on the Germans had Christmas trees to remind them of Jesus.

Queen Victoria's husband, Prince Albert, came from Germany. He brought the idea of Christmas trees to Britain.

## Boxing Day

After Christmas Day comes Boxing Day. Churches kept special boxes for people to put money in. Every year the boxes were opened on Boxing day. The money was given to the poor.

# Pancake Tuesday

In the old days February was the month when people went to church for a special service. They said they were sorry for being wicked. They were <u>shriven</u>.

After that came a very serious time called <u>Lent</u>. During Lent no one was allowed to eat meat, eggs or milk.

The day before Lent began people made pancakes. This was to use up their fats and eggs. The day before Lent begins is still called Shrove Tuesday.

Every year the boys at Westminster School in London still rush to get a pancake tossed by the chef. The boy with the biggest piece gets a prize. Here is a picture of this custom happening about 120 years ago.

# Easter Eggs

Lent ends at Easter. What do you think people would have liked to eat then? One thing they would have liked was an egg.

Giving eggs is a very old custom. It was done long before Jesus was born. The eggs reminded people of the new life that was coming with the spring.

These children are decorating hard-boiled eggs for Easter.

Robert Winter · Christopher Wright · Iohn Wright · Thomas Percy · Guido Fawkes · Robert Cateſby · Thomas Winter · Bates

## Gunpowder Plot

We celebrate Bonfire Night by having a fire and burning a guy on top of it. On November 5 1605, Guy Fawkes was captured when he tried to blow up the Houses of Parliament.

Guy Fawkes and some of the other conspirators. They hoped to kill the King and get rid of the Government.

## Things to Do

A  Find out what you can about Guy Fawkes.

B  Find out about the following:
   *Valentine's Day   Burns Night   Hallowe'en*

C  At Tissington in Derbyshire five wells are decorated with flowers. This is done every Ascension Day. Is there a custom that happens near where you live? What is the custom and what happens?

D  In 1842 William Maw Egley made one of the first Christmas cards. We still send them to each other. See if you can collect some. What do they tell us about life in the past?

E  Find out about a custom from another country.

# Souvenirs

Have you ever saved anything specially? Some people save souvenirs to remind themselves of a happy time. They may save a programme from a football match or a theatre visit.

This souvenir was specially made for children. It is a plaque and was made to remind children of the coronation of Edward VII.

Even souvenirs can be wrong! Two days before the coronation Edward fell ill and had to have an operation. He was not crowned till August that year.

## Royal Wedding

The photograph below shows us another royal event. In 1973 Princess Anne married Captain Mark Phillips. Millions of people all over the world watched the wedding on television.

Princess Anne and Captain Mark Phillips were both interested in a certain sport. This drawing of a souvenir of their wedding will give you a clue. Which sport was it?

## Prime Minister

Mrs Shore is an old lady. She owns this plate with W. E. Gladstone on it. The plate used to belong to her father and mother. 'They used to vote Liberal,' she said. 'There was no Labour Party in those days, only Liberal and Conservative.'

W. E. Gladstone led the Liberals. 'We were very proud of him when he was Prime Minister,' Mrs Shore said. 'We hung this plate up in the hall.' Why do you think this plate was made?

## Festival of Britain

In 1951 an exhibition was held in London. It was the Festival of Britain. The Second World War had ended six years earlier.

The Royal Festival Hall was built in London beside the River Thames. It can still be seen today. It is the only permanent building to remind us of the Festival of Britain. It is used mainly for concerts. Famous musicians from all over the world perform there.

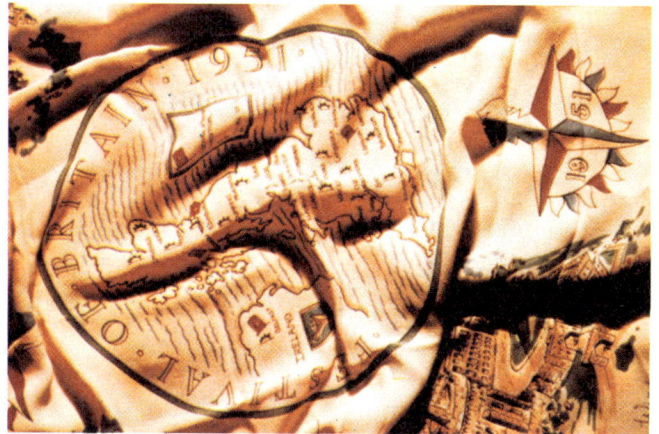

One of the souvenirs of the Festival of Britain. Look carefully for the head of Britannia.

# A Soldier's Souvenir

This souvenir was brought back from South Africa. It is an ostrich egg. Ostriches were kept on farms for their feathers. What do you think the feathers were used for?

The lady is wearing a feather <u>boa</u> round her neck

Compare the size of the ostrich egg with the hen's egg beside it. Which is which?

A man wrote this letter to a soldier. He asked the soldier to bring an ostrich egg when he came home. The soldier was fighting in South Africa against the <u>Boers</u> in 1901. You can see where the letter was almost burnt when a Post Office was attacked in the fighting.

In the end the soldier received the letter and brought an ostrich egg back for his friend.

## Things to Do

**A** Look at the souvenir of the coronation on page 50:
   What were the names of the king and queen?
   How many children in Leeds went to school?
   When was the coronation supposed to happen?
   Why was the date on the plaque not changed?

**B** Pretend your school has been open for one hundred years. Design a souvenir for it. It could be a plate, a mug, a medal or anything else you choose.

# Coins

Roman coin.

Even the money we use tells us about our history. This is a Roman coin. It was used when Hadrian was <u>Emperor</u>. It shows <u>Britannia</u> sitting on some rocks.

## Britannia

Here is another coin with Britannia on it. King Charles II decided to use this design on his coins. The model he chose for Britannia was one of his friends. She was called Frances Stewart. We still use her picture on some of our coins today. Can you find one?

The 50p piece replaced the 10 shilling note in old money.

## Prince of Wales

This is a two pence piece. The feathers on it are called the 'Prince of Wales Feathers'.

There is a story (which may not be true) that the Prince of Wales first saw them at the Battle of Crecy, about six hundred years ago.

King John of Bohemia had them on his shield. He was fighting for the French, even though he was blind. Prince Edward, the Prince of Wales, thought he was very brave. When the blind king was killed, Edward took the feathers for his own shield.

Edward's tomb in Canterbury Cathedral. He is sometimes called the Black Prince.

## St Edward's Crown

Look at the picture of the Archbishop crowning the Queen. He has placed the crown on her head. You can see the same crown on a half pence piece. It is called St Edward's Crown. The crown is very heavy. During the service it is changed for another crown. King Charles II had St Edward's Crown made because the old crown had disappeared in 1649.

## The Tudor Crown

The crown on the one penny piece is different. It was part of the coat-of-arms of the Tudor family. Elizabeth I was a Tudor. What else do you see on the coin?

## The Golden Hind

This coin is an old halfpenny. The ship on it is the *Golden Hind*. Sir Francis Drake changed its name from the *Pelican* when he sailed round the world in it. The voyage took from 1577 to 1580. Drake was one of Elizabeth I's great seamen.

Queen Elizabeth II being crowned in Westminster Abbey in June 1953.

The *Golden Hind*.

# The Jubilee Crown

This is a special coin. It was made for Queen Elizabeth II's Silver Jubilee. It is called a crown. It was worth 25p. On one side you can see the Queen riding her horse. What can you see on the other side? The St Edward's Crown may give you a clue what they were used for.

**A** Find out more about:

*Emperor Hadrian*　　　*King Charles II*　　　*The Black Prince*　　　*Elizabeth I*

**B** Write out and complete the following sentences:
(The pictures on the right may help you.)

1. The design on a two pence piece is called ....
2. The face of Frances Stewart is found on ....
3. The design in the centre of a ten pence piece is a ....
4. The crown on a half pence piece is called ....

**C** Look again at the one pence piece. The gate on it is called a portcullis. Where were these used? What do you think the chains on the portcullis were for?

**D** The Crown Jewels are kept in the Tower of London. Make a cardboard model of them. (You will probably find pictures of them in books in your school library.) Label each item and say what it is for. The *Children's Britannica* will help you.

**E** Design a coin to be used instead of either the £5 note or the £10 note.

# The Day After Tomorrow

Jules Verne was a writer. In 1865 he wrote a story about some men who went to the moon. Many people thought his story foolish.

In 1902 George Melies made a film about going to the moon. People said he was foolish too, because nobody could possibly go there.

But Jules Verne and George Melies were right. Men did reach the moon.

Jules Verne, who wrote *From the Earth to the Moon.*

Scene from George Melies' film.

On the moon. One of the American astronauts in the moon buggy.

# When I Grow Up

It is fun to look forward and guess what the future will be like. The newspaper article on the right did that. It was written in 1954. The writer said what he thought it would be like to live in the 1980s. The boy in the picture is Prince Charles.

Was the author right? Some of his guesses are very good. Concorde can fly to the USA in only four hours.

Concorde – the world's fastest airliner.

## Things to Do

**A** Write down something the newspaper writer was right about, and something he was wrong about to do with

*health work leisure travel*

**B** What do you think life will be like in 2000? Think of the things the writer said in 1954.

**C** Of all the things you have read in this book which would you most like to see? Why?

*The Daily Herald* is no longer published. Can you think of any other newspaper or magazine that no longer exists?

# Quiz

1. Whose tomb did Howard Carter discover?

2. What kind of things would you find in a Roman butcher's shop?

3. Who was the British Prime Minister during World War Two?

4. What happened at Dunkirk?

5. How did Alexander Fleming discover penicillin?

6. Where in a park would you expect to hear a band playing?

7. What is a charabanc?

8. How did the 'pen knife' get its name?

9. What was a cooper?

10. Who introduced the penny post?

11. What does 'Mac' before a name mean?

12. Where does the word 'sandwich' some from?

13. When did electric cookers become popular?

14. Who were the Beatles?

15. When did men first land on the moon?

16. What was the 'Death Cart' for?

17. Where did potatoes first come from?

18. How did people in the Middle Ages prevent meat going bad?

19. What did Clarence Birdseye discover?

20. Who brought the Christmas tree to Britain?

21. What was 'Boxing Day'?

22. What is the crown used at the Coronation called?

23. Where was the Boer War fought?

24. What was a feather boa?

25. Who wrote the book *From the Earth to the Moon?*

# Glossary

| | | |
|---|---|---|
| **evacuated** | taken from a place for safety | 5 |
| **exhibition** | a public show | 17 |
| **expert** | a skilled person | 2 |
| **extension** | an enlargement | 3 |
| **Family Bible** | a large Bible where family records were kept | 10 |
| **Far East** | countries from India eastwards | 6 |
| **Festival of Britain** | a display of British goods in 1951 | 17 |
| **fodder** | food for animals | 15 |
| **gambling** | playing for money, betting | 13 |
| **gas mask** | a face mask to protect people from poison gas | 5 |
| **graze** | feed on grass | 14 |
| **guinea** | 105 pence | 4 |
| **halfpenny** | half an old penny – equal to about half a modern half-pence | 18 |
| **highwayman** | a man who robbed travellers on the roads | 11 |
| **hoop** | a band of wood or metal shaped like a circle, a child's toy | 8 |
| **horn** | an instrument which makes a noise of warning on cars | 9 |
| **identity card** | a card to prove who a person was | 5 |
| **infectious** | disease which can be caught from someone else | 19 |
| **insurance** | a payment in case of accident | 15 |
| **international** | world-wide | 19 |
| **invade** | enter another country in wartime (usually done by armies) | 6 |
| **invention** | discovery | 13 |
| **Jubilee** | a celebration every 25 years | 18 |
| **labourer** | a man who works at an unskilled job | 14 |
| **leisure** | spare time | 19 |
| **Lent** | period of time in the Church before Easter | 16 |
| **lunar module** | small space ship used to land on the moon from main rocket | 4 |
| **mackintosh** | waterproof coat | 13 |
| **mail coach** | horse-drawn coach used for carrying letters and parcels | 11 |
| **microphone** | an instrument which picks up sounds for radio and television | 7 |
| **old money** | pounds, shillings and pence, last used in 1971 | 4 |
| **pagans** | non-Christians or heathens | 16 |
| **papyrus** | plant used by ancient Egyptians to make paper | 4 |
| **pattens** | worn to protect shoes in snowy weather | 10 |
| **pedestrians** | people who walk | 13 |
| **penicillin** | drug used to kill germs | 1 |
| **perforated** | partly cut | 11 |

# Index